SWEET DREAMS Journal

PROMPTS & RITUALS TO RECORD, DECODE & REFLECT ON THE MEANING BEHIND YOUR DREAMS

The Hay House Editors

HAY HOUSE

HAY HOUSE, INC.
Carlsbad, California • New York City
London • Sydney • New Delhi

INTRODUCTION

WELCOME TO YOUR DREAMS

Each night we visit a realm where magic is possible. Where you can meet yourself or anyone else—living, dead, or celestial. Where everything we see is there for a reason. Where experiences can feel more powerful and real than waking life. For all these reasons and countless more, people have sought to unravel the meaning of their dreams since the dawn of humankind. We have studied dreams from all angles, from the spiritual to the scientific, fascinated by their strangeness, their beauty, and their enduring importance in our lives: they can teach us things about ourselves that are hidden in the waking world.

In this journal, you'll explore your dreamscape and learn to decode the messages and symbols encoded in your dreams. Each night, you'll learn about a different ritual or practice for dreaming. And each morning you'll record your dreams, which is itself the best thing you can do to remember them and unravel their meaning.

It's important to write about your dreams from a sleepy place. Keep your journal beside your bed, and instead of jumping up and grabbing your coffee, try to stay under the covers while you write. Keep your eyes closed for a little while longer as you hold on to the feeling of sleep, lingering in the liminal space between your dream life and your waking life. Then reach for your journal and try to write in a stream of consciousness way. Forget grammar, spelling, and coherence. Don't even bother trying to write on the lines. With your eyes half closed, just scrawl what you remember without building logic or a story into it. Record how things felt, the colors, the characters, the places, the objects—everything that stuck out to you.

This journaling practice will hone your recall skills, which makes decoding dreams easier. In these pages, you'll find rituals and habits for getting a really good sleep, which you absolutely need to dream deeply. You'll also discover techniques for decoding your dreams as well as common interpretations of dream symbols. You'll look back at the dreams of your childhood, recurring dream themes, and the most powerful dreams you've had so you can get a real sense of your dreamscape and the lessons you can draw from it.

From there, you'll learn to trust your intuition so you can receive messages from your authentic self, your dream guides, departed loved ones, ancestors, and the expansive oneness of the universe that cradles us all. You'll also find ways to ask your dreams for answers to specific questions, to heal in your dreams from hurt and trauma, and to attract the good things you want in your waking life. You can even begin to explore taking control of your dream life in lucid dreams.

This journal will lead you on a journey into that deep part of yourself that connects you to the universe and the wisdom of your higher self. Through all that you discover on this voyage, you'll find the rituals and practices that can give you a rich and revealing dream life for all the days to come.

"THE DOOR TO YOUR HEART AND TO YOUR DREAMS OPENS INWARD."

–Louise Hay

THE SECRET LANGUAGE OF DREAMS: COMMON DREAM SYMBOLS

When you learn to speak the symbolic language of dreams, you can begin to understand the messages, advice, and warnings they are offering you. Here is a list of common dream symbols and their meanings. If any of the meanings given here don't resonate with you, trust your intuition and come up with your own interpretations. Use this list as a reference as you journal, referring back to these common symbols and their meanings to enrich your experience of dream exploration.

Angel: These celestial messengers may bring you guidance as well as make you feel protected and healed.

Being Chased: There is a person or an issue that you're avoiding. Who or what is chasing you can be an indication of what you're avoiding.

Being Haunted: If you are being haunted by a ghost or specter (which is different from being visited by the spirit of a loved one), there may be something in your past that you need to acknowledge and grapple with.

Bridge: Seeing or crossing a bridge in a dream may indicate that you are leaving trouble behind you.

Butterfly: You may be undergoing a monumental transformation. Just as the caterpillar turns into the butterfly, perhaps you are changing into a new, gorgeous version of yourself.

Child or Baby Crying: You have a wish or a need that is unfulfilled and you're crying out for the attention needed to satisfy it.

Children Playing: This indicates that it's time to relax a little, maybe be a little less serious, and enjoy yourself.

Dancing: To dream about dancing by yourself can indicate you're feeling free and happy. If you're dancing with your partner, you might be lusting for them. If your ex is your dance partner, it indicates you're letting go of any lingering feelings for them.

Discovering a New Room: New aspects of your personality are emerging. Embrace them! If the room is old or shows signs of disuse, it may be that some part of yourself that you have forgotten about is resurfacing.

Elderly Person: This could represent a mentor or ancestor with words of wisdom and guidance for you, so listen closely.

Falling: You are likely worried about something that has an element of the unknown to it. You may be afraid that you're losing control of that situation.

Feeling Fear: If you feel fear in a dream, especially if that fear is unattached to something, you may be unsure whether you are doing the right thing in your waking life.

Finding Money: If you are excited about finding money, it can indicate that you feel like you're reaping the benefits from your good work. If you feel anxious and unsure about finding money, this can mean you feel insecure about your resources.

Flower Garden: You are content and happy right now, feeling awash in abundance and love.

Flying: You are ready to break past something that's been holding you back and trust yourself to kick butt.

Illness: A dream in which you're sick can feel alarming, but it's really a kick in the pants to enjoy life, since none of us know how long we'll have it.

Intruder: There is something deep inside you that you have been hiding from and need to reckon with.

Loose or Losing Teeth: This can belie loss or fear of loss. It may also indicate anxiety over an upcoming challenge.

Lost at an Old School: You might feel as though something is lost in your waking life. It can be a person, an object, or even your way.

Moon: If you see the moon in your dreams, you might be feeling like you can't see things clearly right now; you're a bit in the dark.

Naked or Underdressed: You may be feeling unprepared for something going on in your life and afraid that you'll be exposed in some way.

Packing Up: Dreams about packing for a trip or a move show that you're putting away old memories and making room for something new.

Paralysis: Things in your waking life may feel out of control, or you may be afraid to make a decision.

Parents: You may be feeling insecure or lonely, wishing for advice or protection. If you're arguing with your parents, you may be feeling reckless.

Pest Infestation: Finding your home or other personal space infested with insects or rodents may indicate that a molehill in your life is becoming a mountain. It could also mean that you feel like your privacy is being invaded.

Physical Fight: You may be at odds with yourself and dealing with a lot of inner turmoil.

Previous Home: Finding yourself in an old home may indicate that you should revisit that time in your life to learn something important about yourself.

Rabbit: A white rabbit can indicate you're feeling secure in your love life, while a black rabbit may mean you're having trouble trusting your partner.

Running a Race: You likely feel as though you're in a competition, maybe with colleagues at work, or maybe you feel you're competing with someone for the attention of a loved one.

School Locker: If you can't open your old locker, you could be having anxiety about meeting a looming deadline.

Slow-Motion Trouble: If you are in a slow-moving car and the brakes don't work or you can't seem to find them, you may feel that you've lost control over something in your life, or perhaps that you made a choice but now things are moving too quickly.

Snakes: Depending on how you feel about snakes, they could mean transition and rebirth, or they could mean you're afraid of something that feels hidden from you.

Struggling Underwater or Drowning: You may be feeling overwhelmed in the waking world and that important things are out of your control.

Unable to Find a Restroom: Something is likely changing in your waking life and you're feeling unsettled or ungrounded. If you manage to go to the bathroom, that may mean you're releasing some negativity—or that you actually have to pee!

Unprepared for a Test at School: You may have recently suffered an embarrassment that you're not yet healed from.

Waves: You may be on an emotional seesaw as of late, going back and forth between feeling calm and panicked, secure and vulnerable.

“THE MOMENT THAT
YOU ACTUALLY BELIEVE
DREAMS ARE VALUABLE . . .
YOU’LL START TO RECALL
YOUR DREAMS.”

–Leon Nacson

IMPROVE YOUR DREAM RECALL

An important element to decoding your dreams is being able to recall them in the morning. Even the most real-feeling dreams can slip away when you wake up. Writing them down first is the best thing you can do to capture the details of your dreams, but you may also want to try the following practices recommended by dream coach Leon Nacson:

- Go to sleep well hydrated.
- Make sure your bedding isn't too warm. You want to be comfortable but not hot, which can cause restlessness and inhibit dream recall.
- When you're going to sleep, tell yourself that your dreams are valuable and that you will remember them in the morning. Repeat this in your mind several times as you fall asleep.
- Use a gentle alarm to wake you in the morning.
- Don't try to become alert right away. Stay in bed for a little while. Allow yourself to stay sleepy. In this in-between state, you'll be able to remember your dreams more easily.

BEFORE BED *What value do you place on your dreams?*

....

....

....

....

continued . . .

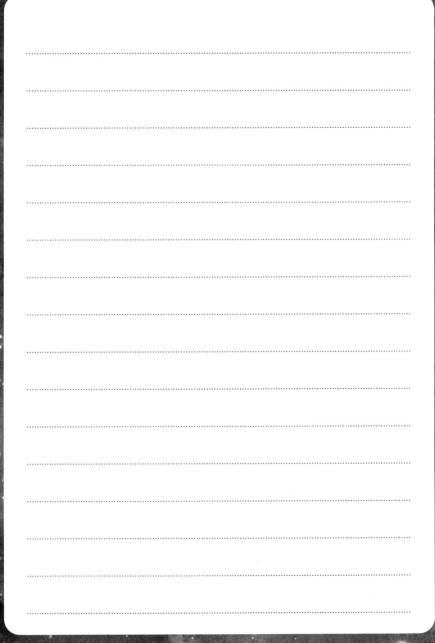

ON WAKING *What did you dream last night? Are you better able to recall your dreams this morning?*

A BEDTIME RITUAL FOR SWEET DREAMS

Having a routine that helps you wind down can lead to better sleep, which gives you more time to dream and makes it easier to remember your dreams in the morning. Reframing that routine as a ritual allows you to experience sleep as a practice and your dreams as sacred. Anything you do regularly with intention and love can be a ritual.

Try winding down for bed at the same time each night with intention. Perhaps set an alarm about an hour before you plan to slide between the sheets that prompts you to start turning off electronics. You might then have a soothing cup of tea, take a warm bath or shower, listen to restful music, read a book, meditate, stretch, or of course journal.

BEFORE BED *What routines do you usually follow before bed? Is there a ritual you'd like to add?*

ON WAKING *What did you dream last night?*

A CLEAN NIGHT'S SLEEP

Where you dream can have a significant impact on what you dream. Make your bed with clean bedding that is right for the season, wear comfy pajamas that you don't get tangled in, make sure your room is truly dark and reasonably neat. As part of your bedtime ritual, you can diffuse a calming essential oil such as lavender or chamomile or find a spray intended for linens that has these soothing scents. All this sets the scene for the kind of deep sleep that opens you to vivid dreams and clear messages.

BEFORE BED *Describe your bedroom. What could you change about it to make it more comfortable and restful?*

ON WAKING *What did you dream last night? What do you think your dream was trying to tell you?*

DAYDREAMING

You don't dream only when you're asleep. Daydreams happen when you allow your thoughts to wander and your imagination to come to life. Maybe you let daydreams go where they like, or perhaps you help direct them a little. Just like dreaming at night, daydreams can be fun, adventurous, sexy, magical, or even stressful. Regardless of where they go, allowing yourself to daydream helps you untangle problems, process your day, and receive messages from deep down or way out.

Why don't you try a little daydreaming now with this coloring page? Allow your thoughts to drift to things that bring you joy, something you're looking forward to, or a treasured memory as you allow your intuition to guide your coloring.

Let your mind wander through daydreams as you color this page.

GET IT OUT

Taking your day to bed with you can make it difficult to fall asleep and cause you to be restless during the night. Spend a few minutes writing down whatever is on your mind or bothering you. This can help you let go of your worries and your to-do list for the night, provide some mental clarity, and make space for deeper, more meaningful dreaming.

BEFORE BED *What do you want to get off your mind before you go to sleep tonight?*

ON WAKING *What did you dream last night? Did you notice any difference in your sleep or dreams after writing down your worries?*

YOUR CALM PLACE

Meditating when you get into bed can help quiet the chatter of the mind so you can better hear the messages your dreams are trying to communicate to you. One simple visualization meditation you can try is picturing a calm place in nature. It can be a real place you really love—like a shady tree in your childhood backyard—or one found only in your imagination. Try to give it as much detail as you can. Envision not only what it looks like but also the sounds and smells you notice and the feel of the sun on your face or the earth beneath your feet.

BEFORE BED *Draw your calm place here to help further quiet your mind. Then go there when you lie down to sleep.*

ON WAKING *What did you dream last night? Did you visit your calm place or sleep or dream differently than usual?*

RESTFUL BODY, DEEPER DREAMS

One way to calm your mind and body for a restful and receptive night of dreaming is through progressive muscle relaxation. When you get into bed, start at either the top of your head or the tip of your toes, and then flex and relax the muscles of your body, one at a time. Bring attention to each toe, each muscle, each part you can think of, one by one. Flex and relax each one in turn. Notice any sensations or tension and send some love and care to every part. You might not even get through your whole body before you fall into a deep, dream-filled sleep.

BEFORE BED *In the space below, write a list of places in your body where you are experiencing aches or soreness. Color in the diagram of your muscles on the next page, using specific colors for places that hold tension or that you want to send more love to.*

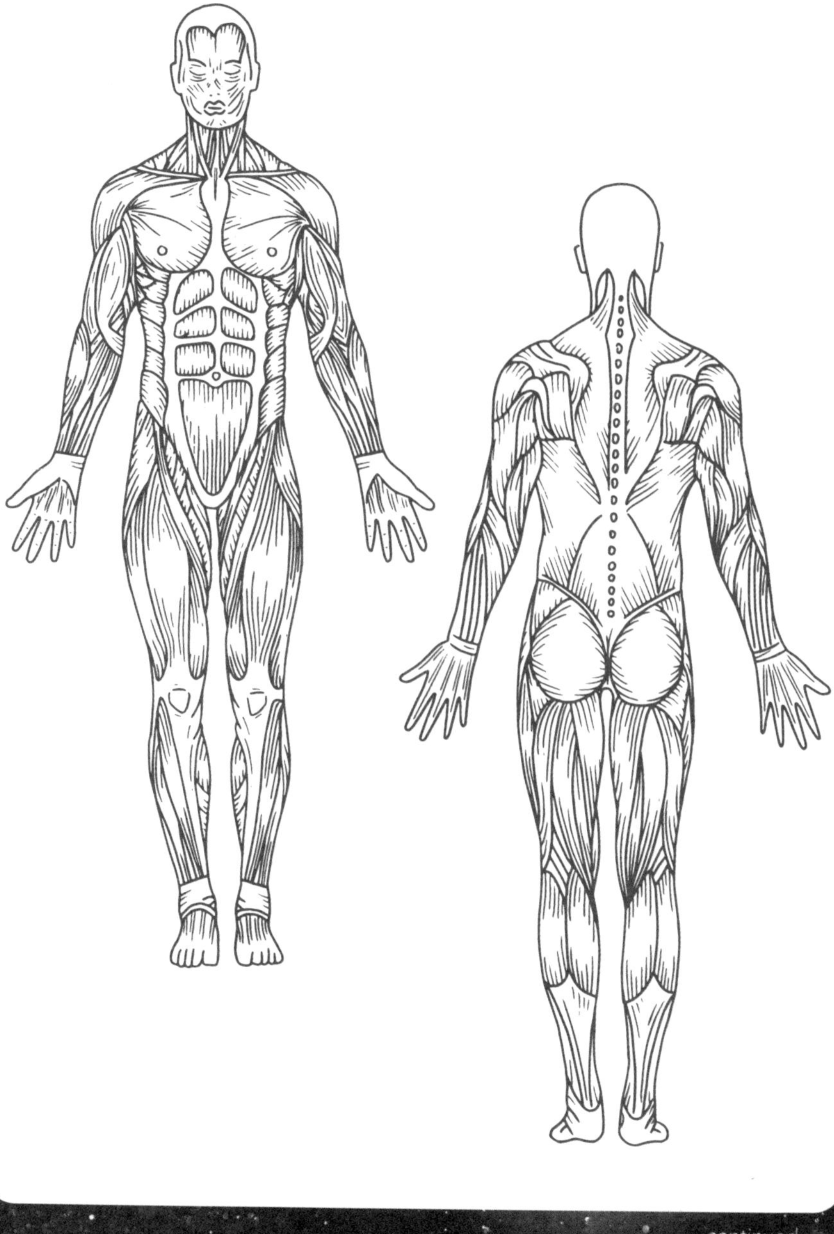

continued . . .

ON WAKING *What did you dream last night? Does your body feel rested? Did you dream more deeply?*

BREATHE IN BETTER SLEEP

By connecting to your breath, you connect with your own life force and all of life around you. When you foster this connection as you fall asleep, you can clear a path for messages and guides to reach you in your dreams. Try this breathing exercise.

After you're in bed, cozy and comfy, close your eyes and bring your awareness to your breath. Feel it as it comes in through your nostrils, gently fills your lungs, and then softly escapes through your mouth or nose. Slowly count up to three as you inhale, pause at the top of your breath, then exhale as you count to five. No need to inhale super deeply or make this at all challenging. Try to breathe normally, and if that means adjusting what you count to, that's totally fine. If your thoughts wander, bring them back to your breath, enjoying the soothing rhythm of breathing until you drift off to sleep.

BEFORE BED *Focus on your breath as you color the scene on the following page, allowing yourself to make intuitive choices, concentrating not on the end result but on the experience of coloring.*

continued . . .

ON WAKING *What did you dream last night? Do you feel the breathing exercise cleared a path for messages or guides to reach you in your dreams?*

DECODING YOUR DREAMS

Dreams are windows into your deepest self. When you're in them, your conscious mind drops away, allowing you to more easily connect not only to your past, present, and future selves but also to the universal energy, so you may receive messages from your higher self, your soul, and even spirit beings, deceased loved ones, and ancestors.

To decode the meaning and messages in your dreams, you must learn to speak their language, which is not communicated in words alone. Dreams speak in symbols, in emotions, in scenes, and you learn to understand them when you learn to trust your imagination and your intuition. Psychologists and spiritualists alike have offered interpretations for dream scenarios and symbols, many of which we explore in this journal. While those suggested meanings may be helpful, know that the truth is in you. You just need to listen for it.

BEFORE BED *Below, list some symbols that often appear in your dreams, and look them up in the symbol guide at the start of this journal. Reflect on how you feel about them as you go to sleep tonight.*

ON WAKING *What did you dream last night? What symbols appeared? How did you feel about them?*

DREAM LIKE JOAN OF ARC

Joan of Arc was just 13 when the Archangel Michael appeared to her in a garden. She felt he was more real than the flowers and trees around her or anything she'd known. Angels and saints continued to visit her in the years to come, and she believed in them so deeply that when her angels told her to go to the royal court and tell them she'd lead France's army in the long, drawn-out Hundred Years' War against England, she did. And they listened to her. The prince put her in charge of the army, which she led to a victory that would turn the war in France's favor.

Joan was then captured by pro-English French forces and tried for witchcraft and heresy for her holy dreams. So powerful was her conviction in her angels and the voice of her own soul that even as she died, she said, "I am unafraid. I was born to do this."

Joan's story has come down to us through the centuries because it shows the power we have in us if we just learn to hear that guiding voice in our soul. Meggan Watterson, in her meditation *How to Dream Like Joan of Arc*, poses the question: "What is the most powerful vision for my life?" Try repeating that question to yourself tonight as you fall asleep.

BEFORE BED *What is the most powerful vision in your life? Even if you are not sure, write the feelings and thoughts that come to mind when you ask yourself this question.*

ON WAKING *What did you dream last night? What symbols appeared? What do you associate with them?*

ASSOCIATIONS AND INTUITION

Since you dream in symbols, it's important to find out what those symbols mean to you. The suggested associations you find in this journal and elsewhere may ring true or put you on the path to understanding, but to really interpret the symbols in your dreams, you have to uncover your own associations.

BEFORE BED *Draw a symbol you often see in your dreams. It could be a color, a recurring action, a mood, a certain room, a word, a setting, anything. Then try some free association, writing down any words, feelings, or impulses that come to you when you meditate on the symbol. Try not to think; instead, trust your intuition and imagination.*

ON WAKING *What did you dream last night? What symbols appeared? What do you associate with them?*

THE WHO'S WHO OF DREAMS

When people show up in your dreams, they may represent other people, they may carry messages, or they may symbolize a part of yourself. To learn more about why a person is appearing in your dreams and understand their message, think about your relationship to them. Do you know them in your waking life, or are you dreaming of a celebrity or historical figure? Then consider how you felt toward that person during your dream. What do you associate with them? Did they feel like part of you, were they familiar, or did they feel very other?

BEFORE BED *Who are some frequent guest stars in your dreams? How do you feel about them?*

ON WAKING *What did you dream last night? Who came to you? What do you think their message was?*

TURNING THE KEY

The master key to decoding dreams is understanding what the symbols in your dreams represent to you, but to turn that key and unlock the meaning of your dreams, you must also consider how you feel about those symbols in your dreams. That emotional connection is where the power truly lies. Your old elementary school may symbolize your childhood or maybe your potential, but did you feel safe and joyful in the dream, or did you feel lost and scared? In each case, those are very similar dreams telling you very different things.

BEFORE BED *What emotions come up most often in your dreams? What do you think their message is?*

ON WAKING *What did you dream last night? What emotions came through most strongly?*

TRUST YOURSELF

Your dreams are just that: yours. So you can trust yourself to decode them. They are your inner self, your soul's way of processing your waking world, guiding you and keeping you balanced. Honing your dream recall skills, understanding your symbols, and recognizing your feelings all have their role to play. And you bring them together by simply asking yourself, *What is this dream trying to tell me?* Then trust your intuition. You already know the answer.

BEFORE BED *Think about a recent dream that has stayed with you. What did you initially think it was trying to tell you? Do you feel you misinterpreted it, now that you have a greater understanding of dreams, or was your gut instinct correct?*

ON WAKING *What did you dream last night? What do you think your dream was trying to tell you?*

YOUR DREAMSCAPE

Even though we all share a common dream language of symbols and themes, each of us has a unique dreamscape, shaped by our personal experiences and preferences and perceptions of the world. The fabric of your dreamscape—the way it feels, looks, sounds, and moves—is something that you and you alone will know. And while each night your dreams are different, that dreamscape—the world in which your dreams take place—likely feels similar night after night.

BEFORE BED *What is your dreamscape usually like? Do you dream in first person or look on your dreams from the outside? Or both? Do you dream in black-and-white or color? Are images clear or hazy? Are your dreams noisy? Are they short and wild or long and continuous? Do your best to describe what it's like for you when you dream.*

ON WAKING *What did you dream last night? Did your dreams happen in your usual dreamscape, or did they feel different?*

"CHILDREN SEE MAGIC BECAUSE THEY LOOK FOR IT."

–Christopher Moore

THE DREAMSCAPE OF YOUR CHILDHOOD

As children we are deeply connected to the world of our imagination, and the dreams we have then can have a big impact on us later in life. Often children are more open to the magic and messages of their dreams than most adults are—that is, until they're told enough times, "It was just a dream." Of course, that's comforting when it comes to nightmares, but it does stop us from believing in the power and significance of our dreams.

BEFORE BED *What do you remember about the dreams you had as a child? Do you remember how you felt about your dreams? Can you recall any specific dreams or messages you received? Write about whatever left the biggest impression.*

continued . . .

ON WAKING *What did you dream last night? Did thinking back to your childhood dreams before you went to sleep affect how you dreamed?*

MEET YOUR DREAM GUIDE

If you're having trouble accessing the messages from your dreams, a guide can help. It can be anyone or any spirit—a person past or present, an animal, an angel, a goddess—and you can meet them using a visualization meditation before you go to sleep. The following such meditation is adapted from Kathleen Webster O'Malley's *Dream Recall, Incubation, and Healing*. You can read it and then walk yourself through it as you lie down with your eyes closed, or you can record yourself reading it aloud slowly and then play it back. Write about your experience right after your meditation, or, if you fall asleep, reflect on it in the morning.

Lie down comfortably with your eyes closed. Rest your hands at your sides, palms up, hands open, showing the universe you're receptive to what it wants to tell you. Allow yourself to relax deeply.

Open your heart to something bigger than yourself and allow it to connect to a higher power. Breathe in slowly through your heart so your breath can circulate through your body and nourish you. Do this a few times.

Now picture you are lying on a comfy blanket in a beautiful field of flowers where you feel safe, guarded, and protected. It is dusk.

Listen to the sounds of the approaching night—the breeze rustling the grass, the insects humming. Smell the sweetness of the flowers.

continued . . .

Feel the calm as you watch the purple night sky fade to indigo and then to black as pinpricks of stars appear. A shooting star crosses the sky and you make a wish.

Imagine yourself falling asleep. Allow images to appear in your mind's eye as you drift off. You notice you have a visitor. This is your guide.

Look around. Where are you with the guide? Are you still in the field, or are you somewhere else? How does it feel to be with the guide?

Ask the guide if they have a message for you. Listen.

Say good-bye to your guide and ask if they have any parting words for you.

Allow the dreamscape to fade away as you drift off to sleep or as you come to waking awareness.

BEFORE BED *In your visualization meditation, what did you wish for when you saw the shooting star? Who was your guide, and did they have a message or parting words for you?*

ON WAKING *What did you dream last night? Did your guide return with another message?*

BEST DREAM EVER!

Dreams can be filled with so much beauty and magic. You can fly, talk to lost loved ones, receive messages and healing. And while the details of many dreams slip through your fingers when you wake, a really good dream can stick with you. You can remember the way it felt, what it looked like, and what it meant for years, even if you didn't write it down at the time.

BEFORE BED *What is the best dream you can remember? Why has it stuck with you all this time? Did it carry a message for you?*

ON WAKING *What did you dream last night? Did recalling your best-ever dream affect what you dreamed about?*

BAD BUT GOOD

Of course, not all dreams are good ones. Nightmares can terrify us, and anxiety-filled or stressful dreams can put us on edge or make us feel out of control. But even when you find yourself wandering the confusing corridors of a scary dream, you can still look for meaning there. Often dreams that you experience as negative hold urgent messages. They can reveal the truth at the center of a problem, or even what the answer might be, if you're willing to look into the face of what scares you.

BEFORE BED *What is a bad dream you've had in the past? Looking back, did it have any message or meaning for you?*

ON WAKING *What did you dream last night? Was it good or bad? Did thinking back to old dreams affect what you dreamed about?*

MESSAGES FROM RECURRING DREAMS

Your dreams reveal the secrets held by your subconscious mind and maybe even messages from beyond yourself. When you have a recurring dream, it could be that a message is trying to make its way through to your waking self but you haven't been able to hear it yet, or perhaps you haven't learned the lesson it's trying to teach you.

BEFORE BED *What is a recurring dream or dream symbol you have? What might it be trying to tell you or teach you?*

ON WAKING *What did you dream last night? Was it a recurring dream or dream symbol?*

RELEASING BAD DREAMS WITH EFT

Tapping, or Emotional Freedom Technique (EFT), is like a gentle form of self-acupressure that helps you clear energetic blockages in the body. If you find yourself awakened by a bad dream, or if can't shake one you've had in the past, tapping could help you work through the stress, anxiety, or fear that dream was bringing to light.

Start with a setup phrase to articulate the situation for yourself, for example: "I have unresolved issues that are appearing in my dreams. I love myself, and I can release these issues now." Once you have clarified this, create a brief reminder phrase like, "Release dream issues" or "Unresolved dream issues." Check in with yourself here and assess how you feel.

Repeat the setup phrase while tapping on the side of your hand. Then say your reminder phrase as you use your index and middle fingers to firmly but gently tap on energy centers in the illustration below numbered 1-8. Go through this cycle of tapping three or four times, then compare how you feel now to how you felt before the tapping sequence.

Tapping Points

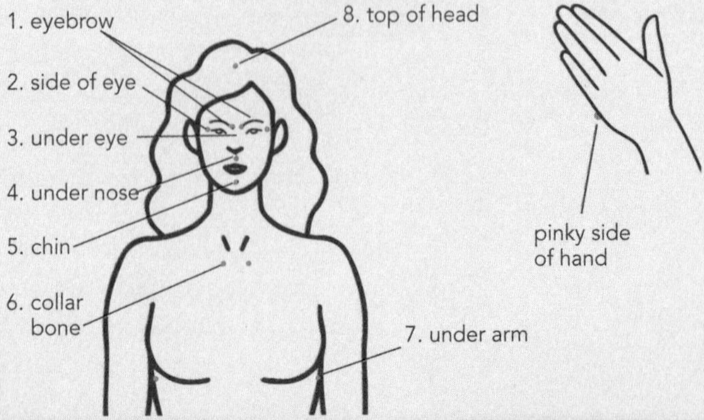

Let your mind wander through daydreams as you color this page.

"FROM EARLIEST TIMES DREAMS HAVE FASCINATED US, AND FOR GOOD REASON. THEY OFFER MOMENTS OF TRUTH THAT REVEAL SOMETHING OF OURSELVES."

–Davina MacKail

DREAM OF AN ANSWER

By focusing on a question before you go to sleep, you can prompt your subconscious mind to release an answer that's been brewing deep in your thoughts but that you have yet to articulate. This practice is known as dream incubation, and people have explored it for millennia, from the ancient Egyptians to researchers at Massachusetts Institute of Technology. People have found it helpful for solving problems, preparing for a big event, or revisiting a great experience. For tonight, you can focus on its power to reveal answers.

BEFORE BED *What question do you want to ask your dreams? Write freely about your question in as much detail as you can, then distill all of that down to a single question you can repeat to yourself as you fall asleep tonight. It's best to keep the question open-ended, something more like, "What is my purpose in life?" than the more practical, yet harder to pinpoint: "What are the winning lottery numbers?"*

continued . . .

ON WAKING *What did you dream last night? As you reflect on your dreams, do you see a potential answer to your question? Remember, dreams often speak in symbols and feelings, not in clear sentences and phrases.*

Let your mind wander through daydreams as you color this page.

A SYMBOL RITUAL FOR DREAM INCUBATION

In ancient Egypt, when people wanted the gods to answer a question for them in their dreams, they would draw on their hand an image of Bes, a deity who helped with childbirth, protected against snakes, and was associated with art, dance, and music. They would then wind a black cloth around their hand, covering the image, and go to sleep without talking to anyone. While the modern world may not believe in Bes, you can try an updated version of this symbolic ritual form of dream incubation for yourself.

BEFORE BED *Think of the question you want answered and try to come up with a symbol to focus your intention—something that captures the nature of the question. Use the area below to sketch out options. Once you have a symbol that resonates with you, draw it on your hand or on a scrap of paper that you can hold in your hand. Then wrap a scarf around your hand and lie down to go to sleep.*

ON WAKING *What did you dream last night? Did an answer come to you? Did you see your symbol in your dream?*

DREAM YOU CAN, AND YOU WILL

If you're stressing out about an upcoming event or challenge, dream incubation can help you feel prepared. Say you have to give a presentation you're nervous about, or you're going to have a difficult conversation with someone. If you incubate a dream where things go really well, you'll likely be more confident and comfortable when the waking moment arrives. You may also do or say something brilliant in your dream that your waking mind hasn't come up with yet.

BEFORE BED *What upcoming experience would you like to prepare for in your dream? Write about it in detail here and then, as you go to sleep, repeat to yourself that you will dream about that experience.*

ON WAKING *What did you dream last night? Have your feelings changed at all about the upcoming event?*

INFINITE CREATIVITY

There is unlimited creative energy in the universe, and you can access it in your dreams. Indeed, many famous creators have said that their dreams inspired their art. Mary Shelley and Edgar Allan Poe wrote stories inspired by their dreams. Musicians from Beethoven to Billy Joel have brought music from their dreams into the waking world. While inspiration can just come to you in dreams, you can also invite it, foster it, and actively step into it.

BEFORE BED *To incubate a dream for creativity, think about your creative passion. Write about why you love it and what it feels like to be engaged in the flow of creativity. Then, as you go to sleep, think of a symbol for your creativity. Perhaps it's a paintbrush, some clay, or yarn. Hold that image in your mind as you go to sleep.*

ON WAKING *What did you dream last night? How are you inspired by those dreams?*

AWAKEN THE SOLUTION

If you're facing a problem and have not been able to find an answer through conventional wisdom, a friend's advice, or any of your other usual techniques, you might be able to uncover a solution in your dreams. In sleep, you have access to your deepest self. If you ask for an answer, you will likely get one.

BEFORE BED *What problem are you facing? Write about it below. Describe how it feels and what's at its core. Then, as you drift off to sleep, repeat to yourself that you will dream of a solution to your problem.*

ON WAKING *What did you dream last night? What symbols appeared, and can you divine a solution from them? An answer might not be clear right away, but reflection can help you see it.*

KNOW THYSELF

Some of the deepest, most powerful things you can learn from dream incubation are truths about yourself. The dreaming you, after all, is different from the waking you. It's freer, more expansive, and has access to so much wisdom and connectivity. Your dream self can find hidden truths, discover the source of a long-held fear, crystallize a vague aspiration, or accept your honest feelings about a troubled relationship.

BEFORE BED *Think about the qualities, values, and beliefs that are essential to who you are. Write about what you feel really makes you you. Try to connect emotionally to your deepest self. Then, as you fall asleep, repeat to yourself that you will learn a deep truth about yourself in your dreams.*

ON WAKING *What did you dream last night? What did you discover about yourself?*

DREAM CRYSTALS

Crystals, with their intriguing structures and natural beauty, are believed to possess and channel energy. Some vibrate on frequencies that can influence dreaming. The following crystals are believed to help people remember and interpret their dreams, facilitate vivid dreams and even lucid dreaming, and ward off negative energies and nightmares.

- Celestite
- Clear quartz
- Dream quartz
- Herkimer diamond
- Labradorite
- Shamanic dream stones (Iodolite)

If you want to bring crystals into your bedtime ritual, start with just one so you can be sure of its effect. When choosing a crystal, let your intuition guide you to it. Before you begin to work with it, you first must cleanse it. You do this simply by setting the crystal on a windowsill overnight during a full moon. Then you can infuse it with your intention by holding it in your hand and thinking about how you want to use it for dreaming.

When you go to bed at night, hold it over your third-eye chakra—the spot on your forehead between and just above your eyes—and visualize the crystal filling you with light as you take a few slow breaths. You may also repeat a mantra if it feels right.

Let your mind wander through daydreams as you color this page.

MEET YOUR ANCESTORS

There are many beings you can meet in your dreams who can offer guidance, messages, and healing. While you can't control who your dream guides will be, you can invite different guides to visit you by using different meditative visualizations before you fall asleep. This meditation is meant to call in your ancestors for guidance, strength, and wisdom. Read it and then walk yourself through the steps as you lie down with your eyes closed, or you can record yourself reading it aloud slowly and then play it back. Write about your experience right after your meditation or simply fall asleep. You can reflect on it in the morning.

Lie down comfortably with your eyes closed. Rest your hands at your sides, palms up, hands open, showing the universe you're receptive to what it wants to tell you. Allow yourself to relax deeply.

Imagine you are walking down a path through a beautiful forest. You feel safe and protected here. A gentle breeze carries the scent of leaves and you hear birds singing. As you walk, you notice the sound of running water. It becomes louder as you follow the path.

As you come around a bend, you see a small river with a stone bridge arching over it. It feels familiar.

You walk across the bridge and as you get to the other side, you see chimes hanging from a tree. Beside them hangs a worn wooden stick. You take the stick, which is smooth in your hands, and run it across the chimes. They ring out in clear, pleasing notes.

Before the last chime ends, you notice a figure approaching from the path still ahead of you. It is your ancestor, and you feel strengthened by their presence.

You ask them for wisdom and guidance, which they give to you. You thank them, and they walk back the way they came as you walk back over the bridge and return to awareness or drift off to sleep.

BEFORE BED *In your visualization meditation, could you see clearly who your ancestor was? What wisdom did you receive from them?*

....

....

....

....

....

....

....

....

....

....

....

continued . . .

ON WAKING *What did you dream last night? Did an ancestor appear? Describe their appearance and what they communicated to you.*

MESSAGES FROM YOUR INNER SELF

So much wisdom and insight live inside you, and dreams can help you unlock deep messages from your subconscious and from your spirit. These messages can help you solve problems, reveal things about you, or add to your creative spark. You can get in touch with your inner self by inviting them to join you much in the same way you invite a spirit guide or ancestor to be with you in your dreams: through a visualization meditation.

First, get into your favorite pajamas, maybe play some relaxing music or spritz a lovely essential oil—do something to show yourself a little extra love. Decide whether you have a specific question you want answered or whether you're just in it for the journey. Then snuggle up under the covers and read this visualization from start to finish. If you easily remember the sequence, you can go through the steps in your head as you lie with your eyes closed, or you can record yourself reading it slowly and then play it back. Write about your experience right after you finish, or allow yourself to drift off to asleep and reflect on it in the morning.

As you lie in bed, cuddled under the blankets, rest your hands over your heart. Slow your breathing and see if you can sense your heartbeat. Drift deeper and deeper into total relaxation.

Imagine you are walking down a corridor. It's cozy and warmly lit as if by many candles. As you walk along the corridor, you notice there are open doors. You approach the first door and you see yourself as you are now. You look happy and peaceful.

continued . . .

You walk on, and through the next door, you see yourself a bit younger. You appear so cheerful and strong. Observe yourself for a few moments.

Then continue down the warm corridor. You come to another door. Through it you see yourself as a teenager. You look so vibrant! Spend some time watching your teenage self.

You continue to walk and are now approaching the end of the corridor. There is an open door there as well. Through it you see yourself as a young child, playing with your favorite toy. Enter the room and give yourself a big hug. Tell yourself how much you love you. If you have a question, ask it now. Stay as long as you like with your child self. When you feel ready to go, let your child self know that you will always be with her, and she will always be with you.

Slowly open your eyes, or allow yourself to settle into sleep.

BEFORE BED *What emotions came up when you were with your child self? What message did you receive?*

ON WAKING *What did you dream last night? If your inner self appeared to you, how old was she? What was her message?*

MESSAGES FROM DEPARTED LOVED ONES

Dreaming about a loved one who has passed on can be moving. It can be joyous to see them again, and sometimes they have a message or wisdom to give you. While these dreams come and go as they please, you can try to summon a dream of a lost loved one if you feel they have something left to tell you. To do this, use the visualization meditation you used to meet your ancestor on page 76, but call on a specific ancestor to meet you at the wind chimes by focusing your energy on the loved one you'd like to speak with. If you have a photo or other memento that is connected to this ancestor, hold it or keep it near your bed.

BEFORE BED *Who would you like to see, and what would you like to ask them? Describe them as well as you can here—what they looked like, what they sounded like, how they spoke, how they smelled, how it felt to hold them or laugh with them—to help bring their memory close to you.*

ON WAKING *What did you dream last night? Did a departed loved one appear? What did you learn from them?*

"DREAMS ARE A WAY FOR US TO WORK OUT THE DIFFICULTIES THAT ARE SUPPRESSED RATHER THAN EXPERIENCED DURING THE DAY."

–Denise Linn

THE HEALING POWER OF DREAMS

When you go through a difficult experience, a common response is to push away the bad feelings rather than process them. Suppressing these experiences instead of dealing with them can create barriers and blockages in your life. Fortunately, dreams give you a safe space to process the hurts of the day or even of your deeper past, and by repeating affirmations while you fall asleep, you can channel the power of your dreams to release that pain and trauma. Simply telling yourself "My dreams heal me" as you drift off to sleep can make a big difference in how you feel in the morning. The more deeply you believe in the power of your dreams, the more powerful they become.

BEFORE BED *Below, come up with your own healing affirmations about the power of dreams. Keep fine-tuning them until you have one that really resonates with you.*

continued . . .

ON WAKING *What did you dream last night? Did you wake up feeling healed from any past hurts?*

MESSAGES FROM THE UNIVERSE

Dreams allow you to connect with so much—the spirit realm, your ancestors, yourself. But all of these things are deeply interconnected, making up one whole. You can open yourself to the wisdom of this oneness when you trust that your imagination and your intuition are capable of revealing it to you. That trust can be built through visualization meditations such as the one below.

Read the following exercise and then walk yourself through it as you lie down with your eyes closed, or you can record yourself reading it aloud slowly and then play it back. You may write about your experience right after your meditation; if you fall asleep, you can reflect on it in the morning.

Lie down comfortably with your eyes closed. Rest your hands at your sides, palms up, hands open, showing the universe you're receptive to what it wants to tell you. Allow yourself to relax deeply.

Imagine yourself walking a path that winds gently up a hillside. It is night and there is a bright moon and many stars in the sky lighting your way. As you ascend the path, you hear crickets softly chirping and you smell the earth.

You walk up and up, closer to the stars and the moon. When you get to the top of the hill, lie down in the soft, sweet-smelling grass and look up into the dome of stars stretching above you, ancient and eternal, divine and familiar. You feel a light in your heart begin to glow and expand with each beat. The light of the stars grows brighter with your heartbeat, matching the rhythm. You are a star now, glowing brightly, connected to the other stars and all that is.

continued . . .

As the stars pulse around you, they begin to form a constellation. A picture. You trust that this picture is a message just for you. You thank the universe for this message as you slowly return to awareness or drift off to sleep.

BEFORE BED *Draw your constellation here. What does it mean to you? What is the story behind it?*

ON WAKING *What did you dream last night? Did you receive any more messages from the universe?*

DREAM HEALING FOR THE CHAKRAS

The chakras are energy centers in your body. When all is well, they spin freely and allow energy to flow throughout you. While there are thought to be as many as 78,000 chakras throughout the body, there are 7 major ones:

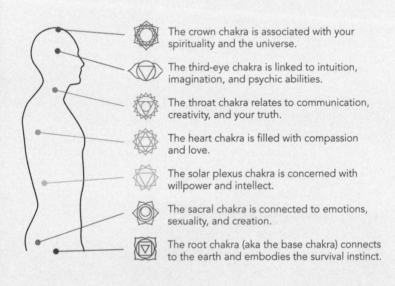

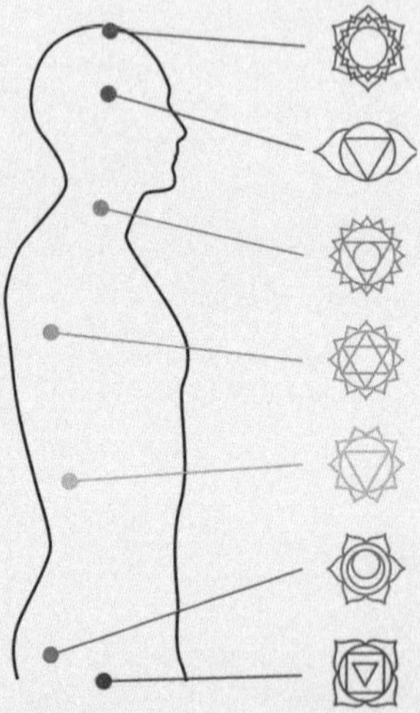

The crown chakra is associated with your spirituality and the universe.

The third-eye chakra is linked to intuition, imagination, and psychic abilities.

The throat chakra relates to communication, creativity, and your truth.

The heart chakra is filled with compassion and love.

The solar plexus chakra is concerned with willpower and intellect.

The sacral chakra is connected to emotions, sexuality, and creation.

The root chakra (aka the base chakra) connects to the earth and embodies the survival instinct.

When one or more chakras are blocked, spinning counter-clockwise, or overactive, your whole system can be thrown off, leaving you sluggish, overwhelmed, or a whole host of other negative things. Tonight, when you lie down to go to sleep, check in with yourself. Scan your body, picturing each chakra as you go. If you like, you can hover your hand over each chakra as you do your scan. See if you can sense how your chakras are spinning, if you're holding tension in any of them. Trust your intuition.

Then, as you drift off to sleep, imagine any chakra that felt off as spinning freely, clockwise, sending light energy through your body.

Let your mind wander through daydreams as you color this page.

THE GREATEST POWER OF ALL

All healing power comes from one source: love. Love means caring, of course, but it also means accepting someone absolutely for who they are. This includes yourself. Many of us struggle with self-acceptance and love, either from time to time or in the long term. But your dream self is the part of yourself that isn't hindered by all the cultural clutter in your consciousness. It is full of acceptance and love that you can tap into.

BEFORE BED *Write down some of the things you love about yourself. Don't be shy and don't be humble. Really toot that horn of yours! Turn those lovely details into simple affirmations. As you go to sleep tonight, repeat those messages of self-love to yourself.*

ON WAKING *What did you dream last night? Do you feel more loving and accepting of yourself this morning?*

DON'T WORRY, DREAM HAPPY!

We all know that worrying doesn't help. It doesn't help us plan or react well or do anything really besides suffer in anticipation of something that may not even happen. Whether you're a chronic worrier or the type of person who worries only when you've got a lot on your plate, it's healing to have tools for putting those bad feelings to rest. And dreams are a great place to use those tools.

BEFORE BED *Write down what you're worrying about. Then take 10 deep breaths—a filling inhale through the nose, and a long, slow exhale through the mouth. As you take these deep, deliberate breaths, cross out your worry. Color over it. Feel it leave you as you settle down for a night of healing dreams and rejuvenating sleep.*

ON WAKING *What did you dream last night? Do you feel liberated from some of your worries?*

SWEET RELEASE

All of us carry baggage from our past. That's not always a bad thing; when you travel, it is useful to bring certain items along on the journey. A map, tickets, a guidebook perhaps. As you travel through life's journey, your experiences impact you and you take those lessons and emotions with you. Some of them are good, some of them are great, and some of them weigh you down. In dreams, we can put down what doesn't serve us, releasing that negative energy into the universe, where it can diffuse and renew into something else.

BEFORE BED *Think of something you've been holding on to that you want to release. Draw a symbol of it below, but leave space around it. Around that, draw some means by which you can send it off—a boat, a plane, a comet, whatever you like. Feel it leaving as you sketch. Then, as you go to sleep tonight, repeat to yourself, "I release what I no longer need."*

ON WAKING *What did you dream last night? Did you wake up feeling a little lighter?*

SENDING OUT LOVE AND HEALING

There are many ways to heal yourself in your dreams, but you can also send that healing outward to your relationships. Often the problems we have with others have a surface story and then a real story beneath—the true source of tension that underlies a petty fight or hurt feelings. These deeper causes can relate to true acceptance of one another, trust, or not fully appreciating the other's experience and point of view. Dreams can guide you to deeper understanding and, through that, healing. Plus, the love and healing energy you wish to send out to the person can travel more easily in the open space of dreams.

BEFORE BED *Think of someone with whom you feel tension and want to send love and healing. Write about your experience with them. Look for the deeper story. Then, as you go to sleep tonight, repeat to yourself that you send understanding, love, and healing to them.*

ON WAKING *What did you dream last night? Do feel you've gained any insight into your relationship with the person you sent love and healing to?*

“WHEN YOU GO TO BED AT NIGHT, CLOSE YOUR EYES AND . . . BE THANKFUL FOR ALL THE GOOD IN YOUR LIFE. IT WILL BRING IN MORE GOOD.”

–Louise Hay

THE ATTRACTIVE POWER OF GRATITUDE

The law of attraction is the belief that your thoughts shape your reality. Having a positive attitude is important not only because it feels good but because it attracts positivity to you. This law has power in your waking thoughts, but in the realm of dreams, where your spirit can more easily connect to the vast energy and oneness of the universe, your intentions become amplified.

Gratitude is one of the most positive and beneficial feelings you can foster, and so meditating on what you're grateful for as you fall asleep is particularly powerful. Counting your blessings at night is an age-old tradition, partly because it can help you recognize and attract more good to you.

BEFORE BED *What are you thankful for? Write a list below, and then, as you fall asleep tonight, fill yourself with a feeling of gratitude.*

continued . . .

ON WAKING *What did you dream last night? What did flooding your system with gratitude before bed attract in your dreams?*

Let your mind wander through daydreams as you color this page.

GROW LOVE

Love really is a two-way street. Often the more love you put out, the more love you attract. It's a balancing force that you can actively grow in your dreams through simple affirmations backed by deep feelings.

BEFORE BED *Bring the feeling of love into your heart. Let it fill you up. Know you deserve love and you have so much love to give. As you do, draw below something that represents love to you: a hug, a pet, a huge colorful heart—whatever comes into your imagination. Then, as you go to sleep tonight, repeat to yourself, "I send out love, I attract love," or another version of this affirmation that resonates with you.*

ON WAKING *What did you dream last night? Did you feel love in your dreams?*

MORE JOY!

The good that you can attract into your life is boundless if you just believe it's possible. Releasing the limiting beliefs that put boundaries around how much happiness you think you deserve or could ever possibly find opens you to receiving all the joy the universe has to offer. But just because that sounds nice and is something you'd like to feel, doesn't mean you believe it deep down in your soul yet. You have to repeat it to yourself so you can move from knowing it might be true to *feeling* it is true. This is something you can foster in your dreams.

BEFORE BED *Think about what happiness is to you. The clearer you are about it, the more powerfully you can attract it. Then, as you go to sleep tonight, repeat an affirmation to yourself that reinforces happiness. "I choose happiness," "Happiness is my true nature," and "I only attract that which brings me joy" are just a few options. Choose one that resonates with you or create your own and write it below.*

ON WAKING *What did you dream last night? Describe how you feel, and try to notice if you feel any differently this morning than you usually do.*

OPEN THE WINDOW

To realize your full power, you have to recognize and seize opportunities when they come your way. And sometimes the greatest opportunities in life are not the ones you expected. They are the windows that open when a door closes. They are the path that feels right even though you've been traveling a different road for so, so long.

When you learn to speak the language of dreams and open yourself up to the possibilities of the universe, you can become more attuned to opportunities in disguise and maybe even create them yourself.

BEFORE BED *What do you see through the open window? Trust your intuition. Deny yourself nothing. Draw it below. Then tonight, when you lie down to go to sleep, repeat to yourself, "An amazing opportunity is coming my way."*

ON WAKING *What did you dream last night? Did you recognize an opportunity you hadn't seen before?*

ACCEPT ABUNDANCE

Abundance can take so many forms: wealth, health, love, creativity, and more. To accept all the abundance that is available to you, you first have to recognize that it is everywhere. So often we cut ourselves off from abundance, because we don't believe we deserve it or there's not enough to go around. But there is plenty for you and plenty for everyone else. When you see things in the world you like, accept that they give you pleasure, whether they're a simple cup of tea or a luxury yacht. Bring them into your daydreams, picturing yourself enjoying what you truly desire. This will attract the abundance you want to you.

BEFORE BED *Envision some things you want. Draw them below. Be extravagant and honest. Then, when you go to sleep tonight, repeat one of these affirmations from Louise Hay: "I am totally open and receptive to the abundant flow of prosperity that the Universe offers." "I am constantly increasing my conscious awareness of abundance." "My good comes from everywhere and everyone."*

ON WAKING *What did you dream last night? Do you feel more ready to accept abundance this morning than you did yesterday?*

ESSENTIAL OILS FOR DREAMING

The soothing smell of essential oils can certainly help ease you to sleep, but perhaps they can also help you sleep more deeply. In that deeper sleep, your dreams may intensify and things like lucid dreaming and dream incubation may become easier. Here are some scents you may want to bring into your sleep rituals.

Lavender is the classic recommendation for sleep because of its calming effect, which can lower your heart rate, body temperature, and even blood pressure.

Rose is another calming scent that can help you relax into deeper sleep.

Sandalwood can help calm the mind, relax the body, and bring you to REM sleep more easily.

Clary sage is believed to ward off the negative thoughts that can keep you up at night.

You can use essential oils by diffusing them, using a linen spray that contains them, putting a drop or two on your pillow, or giving yourself a massage before sleep using an essential massage oil or lotion.

Let your mind wander through daydreams as you color this page.

"THROUGH LUCID DREAMING WE GET TO TRULY KNOW OURSELVES, AND TO BECOME MORE MINDFULLY AWARE IN ALL STATES OF DAY AND NIGHT."
–Charlie Morley

LUCID DREAMING

Lucid dreaming is recognizing in a dream that you are dreaming, and often that means you can take conscious control of your actions and the dream itself—to fly higher, talk to someone specific, visit a sacred space, or even astral project. While many people experience lucid dreams from time to time in their dream life, there are things you can do to activate them. Recording your dreams so you know your dreamscape intimately is a great way to build up to lucid dreaming, so you're well on your way already. If you recognize a dream symbol while you're dreaming, that can trigger lucid dreaming.

The most powerful technique for inducing lucid dreaming is also something you're already familiar with: setting an intention that you repeat to yourself while you fall asleep. For lucid dreaming, you can use something like, "When I dream tonight, I will realize I'm dreaming."

BEFORE BED *What is the first thing you will do in a lucid dream?*

....

....

....

....

....

....

continued . . .

ON WAKING *What did you dream last night? Did you enter a lucid dream state?*

REALITY CHECK

Another way to encourage lucid dreams is to make a habit out of reality checks. If you regularly check to see whether you're awake or dreaming when you know you're awake, you will probably start to do that in your dreams too. This is a gentle way to show yourself you're dreaming, and from there you can more easily take the reins of your dream.

The reality check should be something that you can do easily while awake but that would be hard for you in dreams. Maybe it's reading a clock or text. Maybe it's looking into a mirror or at your hands to see if things look normal. Or you could try pushing on a solid surface to see if your hand goes through it.

BEFORE BED *What do you have difficulty doing in dreams? What reality check do you want to try?*

ON WAKING *What did you dream last night? Did you recognize at any point that you were dreaming?*

KEEP DREAMING

You may experience a lot of false starts when you first try to lucid dream. You might even get so excited when you realize you're dreaming that you wake yourself up. Perhaps this is something that's already happened to you when you've stumbled into a lucid dream in the past. It takes practice to stay in a lucid dream and take control of it, but it can be done.

To stay in your dream, you need to distract yourself from waking up. You can try putting your arms out and spinning in a circle, rubbing your hands together, or going back to doing whatever it was you were doing when you realized you were dreaming. Be gentle with yourself and know that it takes time to harness lucid dreaming.

BEFORE BED *What is a lucid dream you've had in the past? Were you able to stay in it?*

ON WAKING *What did you dream last night? Did you enter a lucid dream state? Were you able to stay in it?*

REFLECTION

You've tried many different approaches to dreaming in this journal. You've developed rituals, learned to hear messages, practiced asking your dreams for answers, and opened yourself to heal in your dreams, to attract the things you want in life, and to lucid dream.

BEFORE BED *Which of these practices did you feel was the most powerful or intriguing?*

ON WAKING *What did you dream last night? Did you use any rituals or techniques for dreaming?*

Hay House Titles of Related Interest

YOU CAN HEAL YOUR LIFE, the movie,
starring Louise Hay & Friends
(available as an online streaming video)
www.hayhouse.com/louise-movie

THE SHIFT, the movie,
starring Dr. Wayne W. Dyer
(available as an online streaming video)
www.hayhouse.com/the-shift-movie

* * *

The High 5 Daily Journal,
by Mel Robbins

Living Your Purpose Journal,
by Dr. Wayne W. Dyer

The Sacred Cycles Journal,
by Jill Pyle, Em Dewey, and Cidney Bachert

All of the above are available at your local bookstore,
or may be ordered by contacting Hay House (see next page).

* * *

We hope you enjoyed this Hay House book. If you'd like to receive our online catalog featuring additional information on Hay House books and products, or if you'd like to find out more about the Hay Foundation, please contact:

HAY HOUSE

Hay House, Inc., P.O. Box 5100, Carlsbad, CA 92018-5100
(760) 431-7695 or (800) 654-5126
(760) 431-6948 (fax) or (800) 650-5115 (fax)
www.hayhouse.com® • www.hayfoundation.org

Published in Australia by: Hay House Australia Pty. Ltd.,
18/36 Ralph St., Alexandria NSW 2015
Phone: 612-9669-4299 • *Fax:* 612-9669-4144
www.hayhouse.com.au

Published in the United Kingdom by: Hay House UK, Ltd.,
The Sixth Floor, Watson House, 54 Baker Street, London W1U 7BU
Phone: +44 (0)20 3927 7290 • *Fax:* +44 (0)20 3927 7291
www.hayhouse.co.uk

Published in India by: Hay House Publishers India,
Muskaan Complex, Plot No. 3, B-2, Vasant Kunj, New Delhi 110 070
Phone: 91-11-4176-1620 • *Fax:* 91-11-4176-1630
www.hayhouse.co.in

SOURCES

Page 6: *Letters to Louise*

Page 12: "How to Recall Dreams," Hay House Radio

Page 46: *Lamb*

Page 60: *The Dream Whisperer*

Page 61: T. Nielsen (2012), "Dream incubation: ancient techniques of dream influence," www.dreamscience.ca

Page 84: *The Hidden Power of Dreams*

Page 100: *You Can Heal Your Life*

Page 114: *Lucid Dreaming Made Easy*